This

Mindfulness Journal

belongs to:

_____

_____

_____

"Mindfulness means being awake.
It means knowing what you are doing."

Jon Kabat-Zinn

Morning Routine

Date: _____

Today's positive Affirmation

```
┌─────────────────────────────────────────────────────────┐
│                                                         │
│                                                         │
│                                                         │
└─────────────────────────────────────────────────────────┘
```

Today's personal Goal
(Write down what you want to achieve for yourself today)

_____
_____

Today's Intention
(Write down how you want this day to be)

```
┌─────────────────────────────────────────────────────────┐
│                                                         │
│                                                         │
│                                                         │
└─────────────────────────────────────────────────────────┘
```

5 Things I am grateful for

#1	
#2	
#3	
#4	
#5	

Mindfulness Exercise
(Notice five things that you can see and write them down)

#1	
#2	
#3	
#4	
#5	

Evening Routine

This went well today

5 Things I am proud of

#1
#2
#3
#4
#5

This made me feel happy

My Thoughts about today

Morning Routine

Date: _____

Today's positive Affirmation

```
┌─────────────────────────────────────────────────────────────┐
│                                                             │
│                                                             │
│                                                             │
│                                                             │
└─────────────────────────────────────────────────────────────┘
```

Today's personal Goal

(Write down what you want to achieve for yourself today)

_____
_____

Today's Intention

(Write down how you want this day to be)

```
┌─────────────────────────────────────────────────────────────┐
│                                                             │
│                                                             │
│                                                             │
│                                                             │
└─────────────────────────────────────────────────────────────┘
```

5 Things I am grateful for

#1 _____
#2 _____
#3 _____
#4 _____
#5 _____

Mindfulness Exercise

(Notice five things that you can feel and write them down).

#1	
#2	
#3	
#4	
#5	

Evening Routine

This went well today

5 Things I am proud of today

#1
#2
#3
#4
#5

This made me feel happy today

My Thoughts about today

Morning Routine

Date: _____

Today's positive Affirmation

Today's personal Goal
(Write down what you want to achieve for yourself today)

_____
_____

Today's Intention
(Write down how you want this day to be)

5 Things I am grateful for

#1	
#2	
#3	
#4	
#5	

Mindfulness Exercise
(Notice five things that you can hear and write them down).

#1	
#2	
#3	
#4	
#5	

Evening Routine

This went well today

5 Things I am proud of today

#1
#2
#3
#4
#5

This made me feel happy today

My Thoughts about today

Morning Routine

Date: _____

Today's positive Affirmation

Today's personal Goal
(Write down what you want to achieve for yourself today)

_____
_____

Today's Intention
(Write down how you want this day to be)

5 Things I am grateful for

#1	
#2	
#3	
#4	
#5	

Mindfulness Exercise
(Notice five things that you can smell and write them down).

#1	
#2	
#3	
#4	
#5	

Evening Routine

This went well today

5 Things I am proud of today

#1
#2
#3
#4
#5

This made me feel happy today

My Thoughts about today

Morning Routine

Date: _____

Today's positive Affirmation

Today's personal Goal
(Write down what you want to achieve for yourself today)

_____
_____

Today's Intention
(Write down how you want this day to be)

5 Things I am grateful for

#1	
#2	
#3	
#4	
#5	

Mindfulness Exercise
(Notice five things that you can taste and write them down).

#1	
#2	
#3	
#4	
#5	

Evening Routine

This went well today

5 Things I am proud of today

#1
#2
#3
#4
#5

This made me feel happy today

My Thoughts about today

Morning Routine

Date: _____

Today's positive Affirmation

Today's personal Goal
(Write down what you want to achieve for yourself today)

_____
_____

Today's Intention
(Write down how you want this day to be)

5 Things I am grateful for

#1	
#2	
#3	
#4	
#5	

Mindfulness Exercise
(Notice five things that you can see and write them down).

#1	
#2	
#3	
#4	
#5	

Evening Routine

This went well today

5 Things I am proud of

#1
#2
#3
#4
#5

This made me feel happy

My Thoughts about today

Morning Routine

Date: _____

Today's positive Affirmation

Today's personal Goal
(Write down what you want to achieve for yourself today)

Today's Intention
(Write down how you want this day to be)

5 Things I am grateful for

#1
#2
#3
#4
#5

Mindfulness Exercise
(Notice five things that you can feel and write them down).

#1
#2
#3
#4
#5

Evening Routine

This went well today

5 Things I am proud of today
#1
#2
#3
#4
#5

This made me feel happy today

My Thoughts about today

Morning Routine

Date: _____

Today's positive Affirmation

Today's personal Goal
(Write down what you want to achieve for yourself today)

_____
_____

Today's Intention
(Write down how you want this day to be)

5 Things I am grateful for

#1	
#2	
#3	
#4	
#5	

Mindfulness Exercise
(Notice five things that you can hear and write them down).

#1	
#2	
#3	
#4	
#5	

Evening Routine

This went well today

5 Things I am proud of today

#1
#2
#3
#4
#5

This made me feel happy today

My Thoughts about today

Morning Routine

Date: _____

Today's positive Affirmation

Today's personal Goal
(Write down what you want to achieve for yourself today)

_____
_____

Today's Intention
(Write down how you want this day to be)

5 Things I am grateful for

#1	
#2	
#3	
#4	
#5	

Mindfulness Exercise
(Notice five things that you can smell and write them down).

#1	
#2	
#3	
#4	
#5	

Evening Routine

This went well today

5 Things I am proud of today

#1
#2
#3
#4
#5

This made me feel happy today

My Thoughts about today

Morning Routine

Date: _____

Today's positive Affirmation

Today's personal Goal
(Write down what you want to achieve for yourself today)

Today's Intention
(Write down how you want this day to be)

5 Things I am grateful for

#1
#2
#3
#4
#5

Mindfulness Exercise
(Notice five things that you can taste and write them down).

#1
#2
#3
#4
#5

Evening Routine

This went well today

5 Things I am proud of today

#1
#2
#3
#4
#5

This made me feel happy today

My Thoughts about today

Morning Routine

Date: _____

Today's positive Affirmation

```
┌─────────────────────────────────────────────────────────────┐
│                                                             │
│                                                             │
│                                                             │
└─────────────────────────────────────────────────────────────┘
```

Today's personal Goal

(Write down what you want to achieve for yourself today)

_____
_____

Today's Intention

(Write down how you want this day to be)

```
┌─────────────────────────────────────────────────────────────┐
│                                                             │
│                                                             │
│                                                             │
└─────────────────────────────────────────────────────────────┘
```

5 Things I am grateful for

#1 _____
#2 _____
#3 _____
#4 _____
#5 _____

Mindfulness Exercise

(Notice five things that you can see and write them down).

#1 _____
#2 _____
#3 _____
#4 _____
#5 _____

Evening Routine

This went well today

5 Things I am proud of

#1
#2
#3
#4
#5

This made me feel happy

My Thoughts about today

Morning Routine

Date: _____

Today's positive Affirmation

Today's personal Goal
(Write down what you want to achieve for yourself today)

_____
_____

Today's Intention
(Write down how you want this day to be)

5 Things I am grateful for

#1 _____
#2 _____
#3 _____
#4 _____
#5 _____

Mindfulness Exercise
(Notice five things that you can feel and write them down).

#1 _____
#2 _____
#3 _____
#4 _____
#5 _____

Evening Routine

This went well today

5 Things I am proud of today

#1
#2
#3
#4
#5

This made me feel happy today

My Thoughts about today

Morning Routine

Date: _____

Today's positive Affirmation

Today's personal Goal
(Write down what you want to achieve for yourself today)

Today's Intention
(Write down how you want this day to be)

5 Things I am grateful for

#1
#2
#3
#4
#5

Mindfulness Exercise
(Notice five things that you can hear and write them down).

#1
#2
#3
#4
#5

Evening Routine

This went well today

5 Things I am proud of today

#1
#2
#3
#4
#5

This made me feel happy today

My Thoughts about today

Morning Routine

Date: _____

Today's positive Affirmation

Today's personal Goal

(Write down what you want to achieve for yourself today)

_____
_____

Today's Intention

(Write down how you want this day to be)

5 Things I am grateful for

#1	
#2	
#3	
#4	
#5	

Mindfulness Exercise

(Notice five things that you can smell and write them down).

#1	
#2	
#3	
#4	
#5	

Evening Routine

This went well today

5 Things I am proud of today

#1
#2
#3
#4
#5

This made me feel happy today

My Thoughts about today

Morning Routine

Date: _____

Today's positive Affirmation

Today's personal Goal
(Write down what you want to achieve for yourself today)

_____
_____

Today's Intention
(Write down how you want this day to be)

5 Things I am grateful for

#1 _____
#2 _____
#3 _____
#4 _____
#5 _____

Mindfulness Exercise
(Notice five things that you can taste and write them down).

#1
#2
#3
#4
#5

Evening Routine

This went well today

5 Things I am proud of today

#1
#2
#3
#4
#5

This made me feel happy today

My Thoughts about today

Morning Routine

Date: _____

Today's positive Affirmation

Today's personal Goal   (Write down what you want to achieve for yourself today)

Today's Intention   (Write down how you want this day to be)

5 Things I am grateful for

#1
#2
#3
#4
#5

Mindfulness Exercise   (Notice five things that you can see and write them down).

#1
#2
#3
#4
#5

Evening Routine

This went well today

5 Things I am proud of

#1
#2
#3
#4
#5

This made me feel happy

My Thoughts about today

Morning Routine

Date: _____

Today's positive Affirmation

Today's personal Goal
(Write down what you want to achieve for yourself today)

_____
_____

Today's Intention
(Write down how you want this day to be)

5 Things I am grateful for

#1
#2
#3
#4
#5

Mindfulness Exercise
(Notice five things that you can feel and write them down).

#1	
#2	
#3	
#4	
#5	

Evening Routine

This went well today

5 Things I am proud of today
#1
#2
#3
#4
#5

This made me feel happy today

My Thoughts about today

Morning Routine

Date: _____

Today's positive Affirmation

Today's personal Goal (Write down what you want to achieve for yourself today)

_____

_____

Today's Intention (Write down how you want this day to be)

5 Things I am grateful for

#1 _____
#2 _____
#3 _____
#4 _____
#5 _____

Mindfulness Exercise (Notice five things that you can hear and write them down).

#1	
#2	
#3	
#4	
#5	

Evening Routine

This went well today

5 Things I am proud of today

#1
#2
#3
#4
#5

This made me feel happy today

My Thoughts about today

Morning Routine

Date: _____

Today's positive Affirmation

```
┌─────────────────────────────────────────────────────────────┐
│                                                             │
│                                                             │
│                                                             │
└─────────────────────────────────────────────────────────────┘
```

Today's personal Goal   (Write down what you want to achieve for yourself today)

_____
_____

Today's Intention   (Write down how you want this day to be)

```
┌─────────────────────────────────────────────────────────────┐
│                                                             │
│                                                             │
│                                                             │
└─────────────────────────────────────────────────────────────┘
```

5 Things I am grateful for

#1 _____
#2 _____
#3 _____
#4 _____
#5 _____

Mindfulness Exercise   (Notice five things that you can smell and write them down).

#1 _____
#2 _____
#3 _____
#4 _____
#5 _____

Evening Routine

This went well today

5 Things I am proud of today

#1
#2
#3
#4
#5

This made me feel happy today

My Thoughts about today

Morning Routine

Date: _____

Today's positive Affirmation

Today's personal Goal
(Write down what you want to achieve for yourself today)

Today's Intention
(Write down how you want this day to be)

5 Things I am grateful for

#1	
#2	
#3	
#4	
#5	

Mindfulness Exercise
(Notice five things that you can taste and write them down).

#1	
#2	
#3	
#4	
#5	

Evening Routine

This went well today

5 Things I am proud of today

#1
#2
#3
#4
#5

This made me feel happy today

My Thoughts about today

Morning Routine

Date: _____

Today's positive Affirmation

Today's personal Goal
(Write down what you want to achieve for yourself today)

_____
_____

Today's Intention
(Write down how you want this day to be)

5 Things I am grateful for

#1 _____
#2 _____
#3 _____
#4 _____
#5 _____

Mindfulness Exercise
(Notice five things that you can see and write them down).

#1	
#2	
#3	
#4	
#5	

Evening Routine

This went well today

5 Things I am proud of

#1
#2
#3
#4
#5

This made me feel happy

My Thoughts about today

Morning Routine

Date: _____

Today's positive Affirmation

```
[                                                                              ]
```

Today's personal Goal
(Write down what you want to achieve for yourself today)

_____
_____

Today's Intention
(Write down how you want this day to be)

```
[                                                                              ]
```

5 Things I am grateful for

#1 _____
#2 _____
#3 _____
#4 _____
#5 _____

Mindfulness Exercise
(Notice five things that you can feel and write them down).

#1	
#2	
#3	
#4	
#5	

Evening Routine

This went well today

5 Things I am proud of today

#1
#2
#3
#4
#5

This made me feel happy today

My Thoughts about today

Morning Routine

Date: _____

Today's positive Affirmation

Today's personal Goal
(Write down what you want to achieve for yourself today)

Today's Intention
(Write down how you want this day to be)

5 Things I am grateful for

#1	
#2	
#3	
#4	
#5	

Mindfulness Exercise
(Notice five things that you can hear and write them down).

#1	
#2	
#3	
#4	
#5	

Evening Routine

This went well today

5 Things I am proud of today

#1
#2
#3
#4
#5

This made me feel happy today

My Thoughts about today

Morning Routine

Date: _____

Today's positive Affirmation

Today's personal Goal
(Write down what you want to achieve for yourself today)

Today's Intention
(Write down how you want this day to be)

5 Things I am grateful for

#1
#2
#3
#4
#5

Mindfulness Exercise
(Notice five things that you can smell and write them down).

#1
#2
#3
#4
#5

Evening Routine

This went well today

5 Things I am proud of today

#1
#2
#3
#4
#5

This made me feel happy today

My Thoughts about today

Morning Routine

Date: _____

Today's positive Affirmation

Today's personal Goal
(Write down what you want to achieve for yourself today)

Today's Intention
(Write down how you want this day to be)

5 Things I am grateful for

#1
#2
#3
#4
#5

Mindfulness Exercise
(Notice five things that you can taste and write them down).

#1
#2
#3
#4
#5

Evening Routine

This went well today

5 Things I am proud of today

#1
#2
#3
#4
#5

This made me feel happy today

My Thoughts about today

Morning Routine

Date: _____

Today's positive Affirmation

Today's personal Goal   (Write down what you want to achieve for yourself today)

_____
_____

Today's Intention   (Write down how you want this day to be)

5 Things I am grateful for

#1	
#2	
#3	
#4	
#5	

Mindfulness Exercise   (Notice five things that you can see and write them down).

#1	
#2	
#3	
#4	
#5	

Evening Routine

This went well today

5 Things I am proud of
#1
#2
#3
#4
#5

This made me feel happy

My Thoughts about today

Morning Routine

Date: _____

Today's positive Affirmation

Today's personal Goal
(Write down what you want to achieve for yourself today)

_____
_____

Today's Intention
(Write down how you want this day to be)

5 Things I am grateful for

#1 _____
#2 _____
#3 _____
#4 _____
#5 _____

Mindfulness Exercise
(Notice five things that you can feel and write them down).

#1	
#2	
#3	
#4	
#5	

Evening Routine

This went well today

5 Things I am proud of today

#1
#2
#3
#4
#5

This made me feel happy today

My Thoughts about today

Morning Routine

Date: _____

Today's positive Affirmation

Today's personal Goal
(Write down what you want to achieve for yourself today)

_____
_____

Today's Intention
(Write down how you want this day to be)

5 Things I am grateful for

#1	
#2	
#3	
#4	
#5	

Mindfulness Exercise
(Notice five things that you can hear and write them down).

#1	
#2	
#3	
#4	
#5	

Evening Routine

This went well today

5 Things I am proud of today

#1
#2
#3
#4
#5

This made me feel happy today

My Thoughts about today

Morning Routine

Date: _____

Today's positive Affirmation

Today's personal Goal   (Write down what you want to achieve for yourself today)

_____
_____

Today's Intention   (Write down how you want this day to be)

5 Things I am grateful for

#1 _____
#2 _____
#3 _____
#4 _____
#5 _____

Mindfulness Exercise   (Notice five things that you can smell and write them down).

#1	
#2	
#3	
#4	
#5	

Evening Routine

This went well today

5 Things I am proud of today

#1
#2
#3
#4
#5

This made me feel happy today

My Thoughts about today

Morning Routine

Date: _____

Today's positive Affirmation

Today's personal Goal
(Write down what you want to achieve for yourself today)

Today's Intention
(Write down how you want this day to be)

5 Things I am grateful for

#1
#2
#3
#4
#5

Mindfulness Exercise
(Notice five things that you can taste and write them down).

#1
#2
#3
#4
#5

Evening Routine

This went well today

5 Things I am proud of today

#1
#2
#3
#4
#5

This made me feel happy today

My Thoughts about today

Morning Routine

Date: _____

Today's positive Affirmation

```
┌─────────────────────────────────────────────────────────────┐
│                                                             │
│                                                             │
│                                                             │
└─────────────────────────────────────────────────────────────┘
```

Today's personal Goal   (Write down what you want to achieve for yourself today)

_____
_____

Today's Intention   (Write down how you want this day to be)

```
┌─────────────────────────────────────────────────────────────┐
│                                                             │
│                                                             │
│                                                             │
└─────────────────────────────────────────────────────────────┘
```

5 Things I am grateful for

#	
#1	
#2	
#3	
#4	
#5	

Mindfulness Exercise   (Notice five things that you can see and write them down).

#	
#1	
#2	
#3	
#4	
#5	

Evening Routine

This went well today

5 Things I am proud of

#1
#2
#3
#4
#5

This made me feel happy

My Thoughts about today

Morning Routine

Date: _____

Today's positive Affirmation

Today's personal Goal
(Write down what you want to achieve for yourself today)

Today's Intention
(Write down how you want this day to be)

5 Things I am grateful for

#1
#2
#3
#4
#5

Mindfulness Exercise
(Notice five things that you can feel and write them down).

#1
#2
#3
#4
#5

Evening Routine

This went well today

5 Things I am proud of today

#1
#2
#3
#4
#5

This made me feel happy today

My Thoughts about today

Morning Routine

Date: _____

Today's positive Affirmation

Today's personal Goal
(Write down what you want to achieve for yourself today)

Today's Intention
(Write down how you want this day to be)

5 Things I am grateful for

#1
#2
#3
#4
#5

Mindfulness Exercise
(Notice five things that you can hear and write them down).

#1
#2
#3
#4
#5

Evening Routine

This went well today

5 Things I am proud of today

#1
#2
#3
#4
#5

This made me feel happy today

My Thoughts about today

Morning Routine

Date: _____

Today's positive Affirmation

```
[                                                                    ]
```

Today's personal Goal   (Write down what you want to achieve for yourself today)

_____
_____

Today's Intention   (Write down how you want this day to be)

```
[                                                                    ]
```

5 Things I am grateful for

#1	
#2	
#3	
#4	
#5	

Mindfulness Exercise   (Notice five things that you can smell and write them down).

#1	
#2	
#3	
#4	
#5	

Evening Routine

This went well today

5 Things I am proud of today

#1
#2
#3
#4
#5

This made me feel happy today

My Thoughts about today

Morning Routine

Date: _____

Today's positive Affirmation

Today's personal Goal
(Write down what you want to achieve for yourself today)

Today's Intention
(Write down how you want this day to be)

5 Things I am grateful for

#1	
#2	
#3	
#4	
#5	

Mindfulness Exercise
(Notice five things that you can taste and write them down).

#1	
#2	
#3	
#4	
#5	

Evening Routine

This went well today

5 Things I am proud of today

#1
#2
#3
#4
#5

This made me feel happy today

My Thoughts about today

Morning Routine

Date: _____

Today's positive Affirmation

Today's personal Goal
(Write down what you want to achieve for yourself today)

_____
_____

Today's Intention
(Write down how you want this day to be)

5 Things I am grateful for

#1 _____
#2 _____
#3 _____
#4 _____
#5 _____

Mindfulness Exercise
(Notice five things that you can see and write them down).

#1	
#2	
#3	
#4	
#5	

Evening Routine

This went well today

5 Things I am proud of

#1
#2
#3
#4
#5

This made me feel happy

My Thoughts about today

Morning Routine

Date: _____

Today's positive Affirmation

```
[                                                                      ]
```

Today's personal Goal   (Write down what you want to achieve for yourself today)

_____
_____

Today's Intention   (Write down how you want this day to be)

```
[                                                                      ]
```

5 Things I am grateful for

#1	
#2	
#3	
#4	
#5	

Mindfulness Exercise   (Notice five things that you can feel and write them down).

#1	
#2	
#3	
#4	
#5	

Evening Routine

This went well today

5 Things I am proud of today

#1
#2
#3
#4
#5

This made me feel happy today

My Thoughts about today

Morning Routine

Date: _____

Today's positive Affirmation

Today's personal Goal
(Write down what you want to achieve for yourself today)

Today's Intention
(Write down how you want this day to be)

5 Things I am grateful for

#1	
#2	
#3	
#4	
#5	

Mindfulness Exercise
(Notice five things that you can hear and write them down).

#1	
#2	
#3	
#4	
#5	

Evening Routine

This went well today

5 Things I am proud of today
#1
#2
#3
#4
#5

This made me feel happy today

My Thoughts about today

Morning Routine

Date: _____

Today's positive Affirmation

Today's personal Goal
(Write down what you want to achieve for yourself today)

_____
_____

Today's Intention
(Write down how you want this day to be)

5 Things I am grateful for

#1	
#2	
#3	
#4	
#5	

Mindfulness Exercise
(Notice five things that you can smell and write them down).

#1	
#2	
#3	
#4	
#5	

Evening Routine

This went well today

5 Things I am proud of today

#1
#2
#3
#4
#5

This made me feel happy today

My Thoughts about today

Morning Routine

Date: _____

Today's positive Affirmation

Today's personal Goal
(Write down what you want to achieve for yourself today)

_____
_____

Today's Intention
(Write down how you want this day to be)

5 Things I am grateful for

#1 _____
#2 _____
#3 _____
#4 _____
#5 _____

Mindfulness Exercise
(Notice five things that you can taste and write them down).

#1 _____
#2 _____
#3 _____
#4 _____
#5 _____

Evening Routine

This went well today

5 Things I am proud of today

#1
#2
#3
#4
#5

This made me feel happy today

My Thoughts about today

Morning Routine

Date: _____

Today's positive Affirmation

Today's personal Goal
(Write down what you want to achieve for yourself today)

Today's Intention
(Write down how you want this day to be)

5 Things I am grateful for
#1
#2
#3
#4
#5

Mindfulness Exercise
(Notice five things that you can see and write them down).

#1
#2
#3
#4
#5

Evening Routine

This went well today

5 Things I am proud of

#1
#2
#3
#4
#5

This made me feel happy

My Thoughts about today

Morning Routine

Date: _____

Today's positive Affirmation

Today's personal Goal
(Write down what you want to achieve for yourself today)

_____
_____

Today's Intention
(Write down how you want this day to be)

5 Things I am grateful for

#1 _____
#2 _____
#3 _____
#4 _____
#5 _____

Mindfulness Exercise
(Notice five things that you can feel and write them down).

#1	
#2	
#3	
#4	
#5	

Evening Routine

This went well today

5 Things I am proud of today

#1
#2
#3
#4
#5

This made me feel happy today

My Thoughts about today

Morning Routine

Date: _____

Today's positive Affirmation

Today's personal Goal
(Write down what you want to achieve for yourself today)

_____
_____

Today's Intention
(Write down how you want this day to be)

5 Things I am grateful for

#1 _____
#2 _____
#3 _____
#4 _____
#5 _____

Mindfulness Exercise
(Notice five things that you can hear and write them down).

#1	
#2	
#3	
#4	
#5	

Evening Routine

This went well today

5 Things I am proud of today

#1
#2
#3
#4
#5

This made me feel happy today

My Thoughts about today

Morning Routine

Date: _____

Today's positive Affirmation

Today's personal Goal
(Write down what you want to achieve for yourself today)

_____
_____

Today's Intention
(Write down how you want this day to be)

5 Things I am grateful for

#1	
#2	
#3	
#4	
#5	

Mindfulness Exercise
(Notice five things that you can smell and write them down).

#1	
#2	
#3	
#4	
#5	

Evening Routine

This went well today

5 Things I am proud of today

#1
#2
#3
#4
#5

This made me feel happy today

My Thoughts about today

Morning Routine

Date: _____

Today's positive Affirmation

Today's personal Goal
(Write down what you want to achieve for yourself today)

Today's Intention
(Write down how you want this day to be)

5 Things I am grateful for

#1	
#2	
#3	
#4	
#5	

Mindfulness Exercise
(Notice five things that you can taste and write them down).

#1	
#2	
#3	
#4	
#5	

Evening Routine

This went well today

5 Things I am proud of today

#1
#2
#3
#4
#5

This made me feel happy today

My Thoughts about today

Morning Routine

Date: _____

Today's positive Affirmation

Today's personal Goal   (Write down what you want to achieve for yourself today)

_____
_____

Today's Intention   (Write down how you want this day to be)

5 Things I am grateful for

#1	
#2	
#3	
#4	
#5	

Mindfulness Exercise   (Notice five things that you can see and write them down).

#1	
#2	
#3	
#4	
#5	

Evening Routine

This went well today

5 Things I am proud of
#1
#2
#3
#4
#5

This made me feel happy

My Thoughts about today

Morning Routine

Date: _____

Today's positive Affirmation

Today's personal Goal
(Write down what you want to achieve for yourself today)

_____
_____

Today's Intention
(Write down how you want this day to be)

5 Things I am grateful for

#1	
#2	
#3	
#4	
#5	

Mindfulness Exercise
(Notice five things that you can feel and write them down).

#1	
#2	
#3	
#4	
#5	

Evening Routine

This went well today

5 Things I am proud of today

#1
#2
#3
#4
#5

This made me feel happy today

My Thoughts about today

Morning Routine

Date: _____

Today's positive Affirmation

Today's personal Goal
(Write down what you want to achieve for yourself today)

_____
_____

Today's Intention
(Write down how you want this day to be)

5 Things I am grateful for

#1 _____
#2 _____
#3 _____
#4 _____
#5 _____

Mindfulness Exercise
(Notice five things that you can hear and write them down).

#1	
#2	
#3	
#4	
#5	

Evening Routine

This went well today

5 Things I am proud of today

#1
#2
#3
#4
#5

This made me feel happy today

My Thoughts about today

Morning Routine

Date: _____

Today's positive Affirmation

```
[                                                                    ]
```

Today's personal Goal   (Write down what you want to achieve for yourself today)

_____
_____

Today's Intention   (Write down how you want this day to be)

```
[                                                                    ]
```

5 Things I am grateful for

#	
#1	
#2	
#3	
#4	
#5	

Mindfulness Exercise   (Notice five things that you can smell and write them down).

#	
#1	
#2	
#3	
#4	
#5	

Evening Routine

This went well today

5 Things I am proud of today
#1
#2
#3
#4
#5

This made me feel happy today

My Thoughts about today

Morning Routine

Date: _____

Today's positive Affirmation

Today's personal Goal   (Write down what you want to achieve for yourself today)

_____

_____

Today's Intention   (Write down how you want this day to be)

5 Things I am grateful for

#1	
#2	
#3	
#4	
#5	

Mindfulness Exercise   (Notice five things that you can taste and write them down).

#1	
#2	
#3	
#4	
#5	

Evening Routine

This went well today

5 Things I am proud of today

#1
#2
#3
#4
#5

This made me feel happy today

My Thoughts about today

Morning Routine

Date: _____

Today's positive Affirmation

Today's personal Goal
(Write down what you want to achieve for yourself today)

_____
_____

Today's Intention
(Write down how you want this day to be)

5 Things I am grateful for

#1	
#2	
#3	
#4	
#5	

Mindfulness Exercise
(Notice five things that you can see and write them down).

#1	
#2	
#3	
#4	
#5	

Evening Routine

This went well today

5 Things I am proud of

#1
#2
#3
#4
#5

This made me feel happy

My Thoughts about today

Morning Routine

Date: _____

Today's positive Affirmation

```
┌─────────────────────────────────────────────────────────────────┐
│                                                                 │
│                                                                 │
│                                                                 │
│                                                                 │
└─────────────────────────────────────────────────────────────────┘
```

Today's personal Goal   (Write down what you want to achieve for yourself today)

_____
_____

Today's Intention   (Write down how you want this day to be)

```
┌─────────────────────────────────────────────────────────────────┐
│                                                                 │
│                                                                 │
│                                                                 │
│                                                                 │
└─────────────────────────────────────────────────────────────────┘
```

5 Things I am grateful for

#1 _____
#2 _____
#3 _____
#4 _____
#5 _____

Mindfulness Exercise   (Notice five things that you can feel and write them down).

#1 _____
#2 _____
#3 _____
#4 _____
#5 _____

Evening Routine

This went well today

5 Things I am proud of today

#1
#2
#3
#4
#5

This made me feel happy today

My Thoughts about today

Morning Routine

Date: _____

Today's positive Affirmation

Today's personal Goal
(Write down what you want to achieve for yourself today)

Today's Intention
(Write down how you want this day to be)

5 Things I am grateful for

#1
#2
#3
#4
#5

Mindfulness Exercise
(Notice five things that you can hear and write them down).

#1
#2
#3
#4
#5

Evening Routine

This went well today

5 Things I am proud of today
#1
#2
#3
#4
#5

This made me feel happy today

My Thoughts about today

Morning Routine

Date: _____

Today's positive Affirmation

Today's personal Goal
(Write down what you want to achieve for yourself today)

_____
_____

Today's Intention
(Write down how you want this day to be)

5 Things I am grateful for

#1 _____
#2 _____
#3 _____
#4 _____
#5 _____

Mindfulness Exercise
(Notice five things that you can smell and write them down).

#1	
#2	
#3	
#4	
#5	

Evening Routine

This went well today

5 Things I am proud of today

#1
#2
#3
#4
#5

This made me feel happy today

My Thoughts about today

Morning Routine

Date: _____

Today's positive Affirmation

Today's personal Goal
(Write down what you want to achieve for yourself today)

Today's Intention
(Write down how you want this day to be)

5 Things I am grateful for

#1
#2
#3
#4
#5

Mindfulness Exercise
(Notice five things that you can taste and write them down).

#1
#2
#3
#4
#5

Evening Routine

This went well today

5 Things I am proud of today

#1
#2
#3
#4
#5

This made me feel happy today

My Thoughts about today

Morning Routine

Date: _____

Today's positive Affirmation

Today's personal Goal   (Write down what you want to achieve for yourself today)

_____

_____

Today's Intention   (Write down how you want this day to be)

5 Things I am grateful for

#1	
#2	
#3	
#4	
#5	

Mindfulness Exercise   (Notice five things that you can see and write them down).

#1	
#2	
#3	
#4	
#5	

Evening Routine

This went well today

5 Things I am proud of
#1
#2
#3
#4
#5

This made me feel happy

My Thoughts about today

Morning Routine

Date: _____

Today's positive Affirmation

```
┌─────────────────────────────────────────────────────────────┐
│                                                             │
│                                                             │
│                                                             │
└─────────────────────────────────────────────────────────────┘
```

Today's personal Goal   (Write down what you want to achieve for yourself today)

_____
_____

Today's Intention   (Write down how you want this day to be)

```
┌─────────────────────────────────────────────────────────────┐
│                                                             │
│                                                             │
│                                                             │
└─────────────────────────────────────────────────────────────┘
```

5 Things I am grateful for

#1 _____
#2 _____
#3 _____
#4 _____
#5 _____

Mindfulness Exercise   (Notice five things that you can feel and write them down).

#1 _____
#2 _____
#3 _____
#4 _____
#5 _____

Evening Routine

This went well today

5 Things I am proud of today

#1
#2
#3
#4
#5

This made me feel happy today

My Thoughts about today

Morning Routine

Date: _____

Today's positive Affirmation

Today's personal Goal   (Write down what you want to achieve for yourself today)

_____
_____

Today's Intention   (Write down how you want this day to be)

5 Things I am grateful for

#1	
#2	
#3	
#4	
#5	

Mindfulness Exercise   (Notice five things that you can hear and write them down).

#1	
#2	
#3	
#4	
#5	

Evening Routine

This went well today

5 Things I am proud of today

#1
#2
#3
#4
#5

This made me feel happy today

My Thoughts about today

Morning Routine

Date: _____

Today's positive Affirmation

Today's personal Goal
(Write down what you want to achieve for yourself today)

Today's Intention
(Write down how you want this day to be)

5 Things I am grateful for

#1	
#2	
#3	
#4	
#5	

Mindfulness Exercise
(Notice five things that you can smell and write them down).

#1	
#2	
#3	
#4	
#5	

Evening Routine

This went well today

5 Things I am proud of today

#1
#2
#3
#4
#5

This made me feel happy today

My Thoughts about today

Morning Routine

Date: _____

Today's positive Affirmation

Today's personal Goal
(Write down what you want to achieve for yourself today)

_____
_____

Today's Intention
(Write down how you want this day to be)

5 Things I am grateful for

#1 _____
#2 _____
#3 _____
#4 _____
#5 _____

Mindfulness Exercise
(Notice five things that you can taste and write them down).

#1	
#2	
#3	
#4	
#5	

Evening Routine

This went well today

5 Things I am proud of today

#1
#2
#3
#4
#5

This made me feel happy today

My Thoughts about today

Morning Routine

Date: _____

Today's positive Affirmation

```
[                                                                    ]
```

Today's personal Goal
(Write down what you want to achieve for yourself today)

_____
_____

Today's Intention
(Write down how you want this day to be)

```
[                                                                    ]
```

5 Things I am grateful for

#1 _____
#2 _____
#3 _____
#4 _____
#5 _____

Mindfulness Exercise
(Notice five things that you can see and write them down).

#	
#1	
#2	
#3	
#4	
#5	

Evening Routine

This went well today

5 Things I am proud of
#1
#2
#3
#4
#5

This made me feel happy

My Thoughts about today

Morning Routine

Date: _____

Today's positive Affirmation

Today's personal Goal
(Write down what you want to achieve for yourself today)

_____
_____

Today's Intention
(Write down how you want this day to be)

5 Things I am grateful for

#1	
#2	
#3	
#4	
#5	

Mindfulness Exercise
(Notice five things that you can feel and write them down).

#1	
#2	
#3	
#4	
#5	

Evening Routine

This went well today

5 Things I am proud of today

#1
#2
#3
#4
#5

This made me feel happy today

My Thoughts about today

Morning Routine

Date: _____

Today's positive Affirmation

Today's personal Goal
(Write down what you want to achieve for yourself today)

_____
_____

Today's Intention
(Write down how you want this day to be)

5 Things I am grateful for

#1 _____
#2 _____
#3 _____
#4 _____
#5 _____

Mindfulness Exercise
(Notice five things that you can hear and write them down).

#1	
#2	
#3	
#4	
#5	

Evening Routine

This went well today

5 Things I am proud of today
#1
#2
#3
#4
#5

This made me feel happy today

My Thoughts about today

Morning Routine

Date: _____

Today's positive Affirmation

Today's personal Goal
(Write down what you want to achieve for yourself today)

_____
_____

Today's Intention
(Write down how you want this day to be)

5 Things I am grateful for

#1	
#2	
#3	
#4	
#5	

Mindfulness Exercise
(Notice five things that you can smell and write them down).

#1	
#2	
#3	
#4	
#5	

Evening Routine

This went well today

5 Things I am proud of today

#1
#2
#3
#4
#5

This made me feel happy today

My Thoughts about today

Morning Routine

Date: _____

Today's positive Affirmation

Today's personal Goal
(Write down what you want to achieve for yourself today)

Today's Intention
(Write down how you want this day to be)

5 Things I am grateful for

#1
#2
#3
#4
#5

Mindfulness Exercise
(Notice five things that you can taste and write them down).

#1
#2
#3
#4
#5

Evening Routine

This went well today

5 Things I am proud of today

#1
#2
#3
#4
#5

This made me feel happy today

My Thoughts about today

Morning Routine

Date: _____

Today's positive Affirmation

Today's personal Goal   (Write down what you want to achieve for yourself today)

_____
_____

Today's Intention   (Write down how you want this day to be)

5 Things I am grateful for

#1 _____
#2 _____
#3 _____
#4 _____
#5 _____

Mindfulness Exercise   (Notice five things that you can see and write them down).

#1	
#2	
#3	
#4	
#5	

Evening Routine

This went well today

5 Things I am proud of

#1
#2
#3
#4
#5

This made me feel happy

My Thoughts about today

Morning Routine

Date: _____

Today's positive Affirmation

Today's personal Goal

(Write down what you want to achieve for yourself today)

_____
_____

Today's Intention

(Write down how you want this day to be)

5 Things I am grateful for

#1	
#2	
#3	
#4	
#5	

Mindfulness Exercise

(Notice five things that you can feel and write them down).

#1	
#2	
#3	
#4	
#5	

Evening Routine

This went well today

5 Things I am proud of today

#1
#2
#3
#4
#5

This made me feel happy today

My Thoughts about today

Morning Routine

Date: _____

Today's positive Affirmation

Today's personal Goal
(Write down what you want to achieve for yourself today)

_____
_____

Today's Intention
(Write down how you want this day to be)

5 Things I am grateful for

#	
#1	
#2	
#3	
#4	
#5	

Mindfulness Exercise
(Notice five things that you can hear and write them down).

#	
#1	
#2	
#3	
#4	
#5	

Evening Routine

This went well today

5 Things I am proud of today

#1
#2
#3
#4
#5

This made me feel happy today

My Thoughts about today

Morning Routine

Date: _____

Today's positive Affirmation

Today's personal Goal
(Write down what you want to achieve for yourself today)

_____
_____

Today's Intention
(Write down how you want this day to be)

5 Things I am grateful for

#1 _____
#2 _____
#3 _____
#4 _____
#5 _____

Mindfulness Exercise
(Notice five things that you can smell and write them down).

#1	
#2	
#3	
#4	
#5	

Evening Routine

This went well today

5 Things I am proud of today
#1
#2
#3
#4
#5

This made me feel happy today

My Thoughts about today

Morning Routine

Date: _____

Today's positive Affirmation

```
┌─────────────────────────────────────────────────────────────────┐
│                                                                 │
│                                                                 │
│                                                                 │
└─────────────────────────────────────────────────────────────────┘
```

Today's personal Goal   (Write down what you want to achieve for yourself today)

_____

_____

Today's Intention   (Write down how you want this day to be)

```
┌─────────────────────────────────────────────────────────────────┐
│                                                                 │
│                                                                 │
│                                                                 │
└─────────────────────────────────────────────────────────────────┘
```

5 Things I am grateful for

#1 _____
#2 _____
#3 _____
#4 _____
#5 _____

Mindfulness Exercise   (Notice five things that you can taste and write them down).

#1	
#2	
#3	
#4	
#5	

Evening Routine

This went well today

5 Things I am proud of today

#1
#2
#3
#4
#5

This made me feel happy today

My Thoughts about today

Morning Routine

Date: _____

Today's positive Affirmation

Today's personal Goal   (Write down what you want to achieve for yourself today)

Today's Intention   (Write down how you want this day to be)

5 Things I am grateful for

#1
#2
#3
#4
#5

Mindfulness Exercise   (Notice five things that you can see and write them down).

#1
#2
#3
#4
#5

Evening Routine

This went well today

5 Things I am proud of
#1
#2
#3
#4
#5

This made me feel happy

My Thoughts about today

Morning Routine

Date: _____

Today's positive Affirmation

Today's personal Goal
(Write down what you want to achieve for yourself today)

_____
_____

Today's Intention
(Write down how you want this day to be)

5 Things I am grateful for

#1 _____
#2 _____
#3 _____
#4 _____
#5 _____

Mindfulness Exercise
(Notice five things that you can feel and write them down).

#1	
#2	
#3	
#4	
#5	

Evening Routine

This went well today

5 Things I am proud of today
#1
#2
#3
#4
#5

This made me feel happy today

My Thoughts about today

Morning Routine

Date: _____

Today's positive Affirmation

Today's personal Goal
(Write down what you want to achieve for yourself today)

_____
_____

Today's Intention
(Write down how you want this day to be)

5 Things I am grateful for

#1 _____
#2 _____
#3 _____
#4 _____
#5 _____

Mindfulness Exercise
(Notice five things that you can hear and write them down).

#1	
#2	
#3	
#4	
#5	

Evening Routine

This went well today

5 Things I am proud of today

#1
#2
#3
#4
#5

This made me feel happy today

My Thoughts about today

Morning Routine

Date: _____

Today's positive Affirmation

```
┌─────────────────────────────────────────────────────────────┐
│                                                             │
│                                                             │
│                                                             │
└─────────────────────────────────────────────────────────────┘
```

Today's personal Goal   (Write down what you want to achieve for yourself today)

_____

_____

Today's Intention   (Write down how you want this day to be)

```
┌─────────────────────────────────────────────────────────────┐
│                                                             │
│                                                             │
│                                                             │
└─────────────────────────────────────────────────────────────┘
```

5 Things I am grateful for

#1 _____
#2 _____
#3 _____
#4 _____
#5 _____

Mindfulness Exercise   (Notice five things that you can smell and write them down).

#1 _____
#2 _____
#3 _____
#4 _____
#5 _____

Evening Routine

This went well today

5 Things I am proud of today

#1
#2
#3
#4
#5

This made me feel happy today

My Thoughts about today

Morning Routine

Date: _____

Today's positive Affirmation

Today's personal Goal
(Write down what you want to achieve for yourself today)

_____
_____

Today's Intention
(Write down how you want this day to be)

5 Things I am grateful for

#1 _____
#2 _____
#3 _____
#4 _____
#5 _____

Mindfulness Exercise
(Notice five things that you can taste and write them down).

#1	
#2	
#3	
#4	
#5	

Evening Routine

This went well today

5 Things I am proud of today

#1
#2
#3
#4
#5

This made me feel happy today

My Thoughts about today

Morning Routine

Date: _____

Today's positive Affirmation

Today's personal Goal
(Write down what you want to achieve for yourself today)

_____
_____

Today's Intention
(Write down how you want this day to be)

5 Things I am grateful for

#1 _____
#2 _____
#3 _____
#4 _____
#5 _____

Mindfulness Exercise
(Notice five things that you can see and write them down).

#1 _____
#2 _____
#3 _____
#4 _____
#5 _____

Evening Routine

This went well today

5 Things I am proud of
#1
#2
#3
#4
#5

This made me feel happy

My Thoughts about today

Morning Routine

Date: _____

Today's positive Affirmation

Today's personal Goal
(Write down what you want to achieve for yourself today)

_____
_____

Today's Intention
(Write down how you want this day to be)

5 Things I am grateful for

#1	
#2	
#3	
#4	
#5	

Mindfulness Exercise
(Notice five things that you can feel and write them down).

#1	
#2	
#3	
#4	
#5	

Evening Routine

This went well today

5 Things I am proud of today

#1
#2
#3
#4
#5

This made me feel happy today

My Thoughts about today

Morning Routine

Date: _____

Today's positive Affirmation

Today's personal Goal
(Write down what you want to achieve for yourself today)

_____
_____

Today's Intention
(Write down how you want this day to be)

5 Things I am grateful for

#1 _____
#2 _____
#3 _____
#4 _____
#5 _____

Mindfulness Exercise
(Notice five things that you can hear and write them down).

#1	
#2	
#3	
#4	
#5	

Evening Routine

This went well today

5 Things I am proud of today

#1
#2
#3
#4
#5

This made me feel happy today

My Thoughts about today

Morning Routine

Date: _____

Today's positive Affirmation

Today's personal Goal
(Write down what you want to achieve for yourself today)

Today's Intention
(Write down how you want this day to be)

5 Things I am grateful for

#1
#2
#3
#4
#5

Mindfulness Exercise
(Notice five things that you can smell and write them down).

#1
#2
#3
#4
#5

Evening Routine

This went well today

5 Things I am proud of today

#1
#2
#3
#4
#5

This made me feel happy today

My Thoughts about today

Morning Routine

Date: _____

Today's positive Affirmation

Today's personal Goal
(Write down what you want to achieve for yourself today)

Today's Intention
(Write down how you want this day to be)

5 Things I am grateful for

#1	
#2	
#3	
#4	
#5	

Mindfulness Exercise
(Notice five things that you can taste and write them down).

#1	
#2	
#3	
#4	
#5	

Evening Routine

This went well today

5 Things I am proud of today

#1
#2
#3
#4
#5

This made me feel happy today

My Thoughts about today

Morning Routine

Date: _____

Today's positive Affirmation

Today's personal Goal
(Write down what you want to achieve for yourself today)

Today's Intention
(Write down how you want this day to be)

5 Things I am grateful for

#1
#2
#3
#4
#5

Mindfulness Exercise
(Notice five things that you can see and write them down).

#1
#2
#3
#4
#5

Evening Routine

This went well today

5 Things I am proud of
#1
#2
#3
#4
#5

This made me feel happy

My Thoughts about today

Morning Routine

Date: _____

Today's positive Affirmation

Today's personal Goal
(Write down what you want to achieve for yourself today)

_____
_____

Today's Intention
(Write down how you want this day to be)

5 Things I am grateful for

#1	
#2	
#3	
#4	
#5	

Mindfulness Exercise
(Notice five things that you can feel and write them down).

#1	
#2	
#3	
#4	
#5	

Evening Routine

This went well today

5 Things I am proud of today
#1
#2
#3
#4
#5

This made me feel happy today

My Thoughts about today

Morning Routine

Date: _____

Today's positive Affirmation

Today's personal Goal
(Write down what you want to achieve for yourself today)

_____
_____

Today's Intention
(Write down how you want this day to be)

5 Things I am grateful for

#1	
#2	
#3	
#4	
#5	

Mindfulness Exercise
(Notice five things that you can hear and write them down).

#1	
#2	
#3	
#4	
#5	

Evening Routine

This went well today

5 Things I am proud of today

#1
#2
#3
#4
#5

This made me feel happy today

My Thoughts about today

Morning Routine

Date: _____

Today's positive Affirmation

Today's personal Goal

(Write down what you want to achieve for yourself today)

_____
_____

Today's Intention

(Write down how you want this day to be)

5 Things I am grateful for

#1
#2
#3
#4
#5

Mindfulness Exercise

(Notice five things that you can smell and write them down).

#1
#2
#3
#4
#5

Evening Routine

This went well today

5 Things I am proud of today

#1
#2
#3
#4
#5

This made me feel happy today

My Thoughts about today

Morning Routine

Date: _____

Today's positive Affirmation

Today's personal Goal
(Write down what you want to achieve for yourself today)

_____
_____

Today's Intention
(Write down how you want this day to be)

5 Things I am grateful for

#1	
#2	
#3	
#4	
#5	

Mindfulness Exercise
(Notice five things that you can taste and write them down).

#1	
#2	
#3	
#4	
#5	

Evening Routine

This went well today

5 Things I am proud of today

#1
#2
#3
#4
#5

This made me feel happy today

My Thoughts about today

Morning Routine

Date: _____

Today's positive Affirmation

Today's personal Goal
(Write down what you want to achieve for yourself today)

Today's Intention
(Write down how you want this day to be)

5 Things I am grateful for
#1
#2
#3
#4
#5

Mindfulness Exercise
(Notice five things that you can see and write them down).

#1
#2
#3
#4
#5

Evening Routine

This went well today

5 Things I am proud of
#1
#2
#3
#4
#5

This made me feel happy

My Thoughts about today

Morning Routine

Date: _____

Today's positive Affirmation

Today's personal Goal
(Write down what you want to achieve for yourself today)

_____
_____

Today's Intention
(Write down how you want this day to be)

5 Things I am grateful for

#1 _____
#2 _____
#3 _____
#4 _____
#5 _____

Mindfulness Exercise
(Notice five things that you can feel and write them down).

#1	
#2	
#3	
#4	
#5	

Evening Routine

This went well today

5 Things I am proud of today

#1
#2
#3
#4
#5

This made me feel happy today

My Thoughts about today

Morning Routine

Date: _____

Today's positive Affirmation

```
┌─────────────────────────────────────────────────────────┐
│                                                         │
│                                                         │
│                                                         │
└─────────────────────────────────────────────────────────┘
```

Today's personal Goal   (Write down what you want to achieve for yourself today)

_____
_____

Today's Intention   (Write down how you want this day to be)

```
┌─────────────────────────────────────────────────────────┐
│                                                         │
│                                                         │
│                                                         │
└─────────────────────────────────────────────────────────┘
```

5 Things I am grateful for

#1 _____
#2 _____
#3 _____
#4 _____
#5 _____

Mindfulness Exercise   (Notice five things that you can hear and write them down).

#1	
#2	
#3	
#4	
#5	

Evening Routine

This went well today

5 Things I am proud of today
#1
#2
#3
#4
#5

This made me feel happy today

My Thoughts about today

Morning Routine

Date: _____

Today's positive Affirmation

Today's personal Goal
(Write down what you want to achieve for yourself today)

_____
_____

Today's Intention
(Write down how you want this day to be)

5 Things I am grateful for

#1	
#2	
#3	
#4	
#5	

Mindfulness Exercise
(Notice five things that you can smell and write them down).

#1	
#2	
#3	
#4	
#5	

Evening Routine

This went well today

5 Things I am proud of today

#1
#2
#3
#4
#5

This made me feel happy today

My Thoughts about today

Morning Routine

Date: _____

Today's positive Affirmation

Today's personal Goal
(Write down what you want to achieve for yourself today)

_____
_____

Today's Intention
(Write down how you want this day to be)

5 Things I am grateful for

#1 _____
#2 _____
#3 _____
#4 _____
#5 _____

Mindfulness Exercise
(Notice five things that you can taste and write them down).

#1	
#2	
#3	
#4	
#5	

Evening Routine

This went well today

5 Things I am proud of today

#1
#2
#3
#4
#5

This made me feel happy today

My Thoughts about today

Morning Routine

Date: _____

Today's positive Affirmation

Today's personal Goal
(Write down what you want to achieve for yourself today)

Today's Intention
(Write down how you want this day to be)

5 Things I am grateful for

#1
#2
#3
#4
#5

Mindfulness Exercise
(Notice five things that you can see and write them down).

#1
#2
#3
#4
#5

Evening Routine

This went well today

5 Things I am proud of

#1
#2
#3
#4
#5

This made me feel happy

My Thoughts about today

Morning Routine

Date: _____

Today's positive Affirmation

Today's personal Goal
(Write down what you want to achieve for yourself today)

Today's Intention
(Write down how you want this day to be)

5 Things I am grateful for

#1
#2
#3
#4
#5

Mindfulness Exercise
(Notice five things that you can feel and write them down).

#1
#2
#3
#4
#5

Evening Routine

This went well today

5 Things I am proud of today

#1
#2
#3
#4
#5

This made me feel happy today

My Thoughts about today

Morning Routine

Date: _____

Today's positive Affirmation

Today's personal Goal
(Write down what you want to achieve for yourself today)

_____
_____

Today's Intention
(Write down how you want this day to be)

5 Things I am grateful for

#1 _____
#2 _____
#3 _____
#4 _____
#5 _____

Mindfulness Exercise
(Notice five things that you can hear and write them down).

#1	
#2	
#3	
#4	
#5	

Evening Routine

This went well today

5 Things I am proud of today

#1
#2
#3
#4
#5

This made me feel happy today

My Thoughts about today

Morning Routine

Date: _____

Today's positive Affirmation

```
┌─────────────────────────────────────────────────────────────┐
│                                                             │
│                                                             │
│                                                             │
└─────────────────────────────────────────────────────────────┘
```

Today's personal Goal   (Write down what you want to achieve for yourself today)

_____
_____

Today's Intention   (Write down how you want this day to be)

```
┌─────────────────────────────────────────────────────────────┐
│                                                             │
│                                                             │
│                                                             │
└─────────────────────────────────────────────────────────────┘
```

5 Things I am grateful for

#1 _____
#2 _____
#3 _____
#4 _____
#5 _____

Mindfulness Exercise   (Notice five things that you can smell and write them down).

#1 _____
#2 _____
#3 _____
#4 _____
#5 _____

Evening Routine

This went well today

5 Things I am proud of today

#1
#2
#3
#4
#5

This made me feel happy today

My Thoughts about today

Morning Routine

Date: _____

Today's positive Affirmation

```
┌─────────────────────────────────────────────────────────┐
│                                                         │
│                                                         │
│                                                         │
└─────────────────────────────────────────────────────────┘
```

Today's personal Goal

(Write down what you want to achieve for yourself today)

_____
_____

Today's Intention

(Write down how you want this day to be)

```
┌─────────────────────────────────────────────────────────┐
│                                                         │
│                                                         │
│                                                         │
└─────────────────────────────────────────────────────────┘
```

5 Things I am grateful for

#1 _____
#2 _____
#3 _____
#4 _____
#5 _____

Mindfulness Exercise

(Notice five things that you can taste and write them down).

#1 _____
#2 _____
#3 _____
#4 _____
#5 _____

Evening Routine

This went well today

5 Things I am proud of today

#1
#2
#3
#4
#5

This made me feel happy today

My Thoughts about today

Morning Routine

Date: _____

Today's positive Affirmation

Today's personal Goal
(Write down what you want to achieve for yourself today)

_____
_____

Today's Intention
(Write down how you want this day to be)

5 Things I am grateful for

#1 _____
#2 _____
#3 _____
#4 _____
#5 _____

Mindfulness Exercise
(Notice five things that you can see and write them down).

#1	
#2	
#3	
#4	
#5	

Evening Routine

This went well today

5 Things I am proud of

#1
#2
#3
#4
#5

This made me feel happy

My Thoughts about today

Morning Routine

Date: _____

Today's positive Affirmation

Today's personal Goal
(Write down what you want to achieve for yourself today)

Today's Intention
(Write down how you want this day to be)

5 Things I am grateful for

#1	
#2	
#3	
#4	
#5	

Mindfulness Exercise
(Notice five things that you can feel and write them down).

#1	
#2	
#3	
#4	
#5	

Evening Routine

This went well today

5 Things I am proud of today

#1
#2
#3
#4
#5

This made me feel happy today

My Thoughts about today

Morning Routine

Date: _____

Today's positive Affirmation

Today's personal Goal
(Write down what you want to achieve for yourself today)

Today's Intention
(Write down how you want this day to be)

5 Things I am grateful for

#1
#2
#3
#4
#5

Mindfulness Exercise
(Notice five things that you can hear and write them down).

#1
#2
#3
#4
#5

Evening Routine

This went well today

5 Things I am proud of today

#1
#2
#3
#4
#5

This made me feel happy today

My Thoughts about today

Morning Routine

Date: _____

Today's positive Affirmation

Today's personal Goal
(Write down what you want to achieve for yourself today)

_____
_____

Today's Intention
(Write down how you want this day to be)

5 Things I am grateful for

#1	
#2	
#3	
#4	
#5	

Mindfulness Exercise
(Notice five things that you can smell and write them down).

#1	
#2	
#3	
#4	
#5	

Evening Routine

This went well today

5 Things I am proud of today

#1
#2
#3
#4
#5

This made me feel happy today

My Thoughts about today

Morning Routine

Date: _____

Today's positive Affirmation

Today's personal Goal
(Write down what you want to achieve for yourself today)

_____
_____

Today's Intention
(Write down how you want this day to be)

5 Things I am grateful for

#1	
#2	
#3	
#4	
#5	

Mindfulness Exercise
(Notice five things that you can taste and write them down).

#1	
#2	
#3	
#4	
#5	

Evening Routine

This went well today

5 Things I am proud of today

#1
#2
#3
#4
#5

This made me feel happy today

My Thoughts about today

Made in United States
Orlando, FL
28 November 2023